Look out!

Written by Erin Howard

raintree
a Capstone company — publishers for children

Have fun ... but look out!

We all like doing fun things. But fun things can have risks, too. If you look out for the risks, you can do all the things you love without getting hurt. Let's start with sport. If you are into sport, you must have the right gear.

Flipping and swinging

When you train to flip, you start out on a thin mat. You train hard – stepping, jumping and flipping. Soon you can do all this up on a wooden bar. But you still need mats.

You can train to swing and twist higher up, too. Keep a tight grip. But if you slip, you will not get hurt with good thick mats to land on.

Teeth

It is good to have something to put on your teeth when you do a contact sport.

Pads on!

For sports like cricket, the bigger the kit is, the better it is. You need a strong helmet and thick shin pads. When you are batting, you might have a chest pad and an arm pad, as well.

Fans have waited all year to see the cup-winners. But with the helmets, the upper arm pads, the chest pads and the leg pads, can the fans see them? Look at them! What do you think?

Winter

For winter sports, you need winter gear – a puffer jacket, scarf, mittens, ear muffs and thick leggings will keep out the chill. And they are good padding if you slip or have a bump. That's a win!

In winter, the sun can still be bright. So, something to screen your sight is good, too.

For winter sports with sticks, you need the right gear and you must look out for the puck. It will hurt if it hits you. The crowd have to look out for it, too!

Tricks at the track

If you go to a pump track or a park to do tricks, you will need footgear that grips. You will need a helmet, and pads on your arms and legs.

At the track, there will be room to do jumps, flips and tricks. You might start by jumping off a little ramp. As you get better, you can go higher. Until you get a trick right, you can expect a slip now and then. Just keep going until you get it. Good luck.

On the river

You have to be a good swimmer to swim in a river. A river might be deeper than you think and the current can be strong. When you put your feet down, look out for rocks. Your foot might get trapped. If you are going to swing or jump in, check how deep it is!
And when you swim, there **must** be an adult looking out for you.

It is fun to fish in a river. You can fish from the river bank. You can go in a boat, too, but put on the right gear. And look out for that sharp hook!

In the surf

You need someone to look out for you when you are in the surf.

This pair are checking for good spots to swim. They look out for rip currents. Rips can drag swimmers out into deep surf.

They mark the best swimming spot with flags in the sand. Then, they keep a look out for risks.

They must be good swimmers. Some have a boat to help them get to swimmers that have swum out too far.

In some spots, they will need to keep a sharp look out for sharks. They ring an alarm if they think there is a problem. There might be shark nets set in the surf, too. The nets let the little fish swim in and out. But sharks cannot get near to the swimmers.

Shark net

Are you a good swimmer? Can you train hard? If so, you might like to help swimmers and surfers, when you are older.

Jobs

Adults need the right gear for the jobs they do, too.

Here is a welder.

A welder joins things by melting flex. She needs to keep a look out for burns. She must keep the hot flex off her skin. To do this, she puts on a bib, thick mitts, a welding hood and a thick cotton coat.

This man's job is near a road. A hard hat and bright top help keep him from harm.

Some jobs are high up in the air.

This picture is from the 1930s. What do you think when you look at it?

No hard hats.
No harnesses.
No nets.
Look out, and do not look down!
You will not see this sort of thing today.

But all was not what it seems. This picture was shot for an ad. The men were not at risk at all! That's good to hear.

Far back, when a tree was cut down, it was chopped with hand tools. Lumberjacks did this hard, hot job.

Today, we have 'arborists'. They have power tools to cut down trees. They still have to look out for lots of risks.

Today's tools are big and sharp. Arborists might get cut by them. So they put on boots, a jacket, pants and a helmet. They might put on ear muffs, too.

When arborists are high up a tree, they put on a harness so they will not get hurt if they slip.

Out at night

If you go out when it's dark, turn on a light and put on a bright top, so you can see and be seen.
Look out – and look cool, too.

Scan the QR code to access the following:
- Information on Reading Road;
- Full details of the phonics covered in Reading Road titles;
- Free downloadable teacher notes and student worksheets for every title.

Quick discussion points

In which sports do players wear a mouthguard?

What protection would you put on to do skateboarding or bike tricks?

Why do you think the author used the title *Look out!*?

What risks do you look out for during your hobby?

Red Squirrel Phonics is published by Raintree.
Raintree is an imprint of Capstone Global Library Limited, a company incorporated in England and Wales having its registered office at 264 Banbury Road, Oxford, OX2 7DY – Registered company number: 6695582
www.raintree.co.uk
myorders@raintree.co.uk

First published in Australia and New Zealand as Sunshine Reading Road
Text and illustrations © Wendy Pye Publishing Ltd 2025
The moral rights of the proprietor have been asserted.

All rights reserved. No part of this publication may be reproduced in any form or by any means (including photocopying or storing it in any medium by electronic means and whether or not transiently or incidentally to some other use of this publication) without the written permission of the copyright owner, except in accordance with the provisions of the Copyright, Designs and Patents Act 1988 or under the terms of a licence issued by the Copyright Licensing Agency, 5th Floor, Shackleton House, 4 Battle Bridge Lane, London, SE1 2HX (www.cla.co.uk). Applications for the copyright owner's written permission should be addressed to the publisher.

Photo credits:
iStockphoto: ©–JulPo: Cover; ©–vgajic: p. 2 (left, right); ©–vm: p. 4 (bottom); ©–stevecoleimages: p. 5 (top); ©–4x6: p. 5 (bottom); ©–ultramarinfoto: p. 6; ©–MiachaelSvoboda: pp. 10 (bottom), 11 (top); ©–abu: p. 11 (bottom); ©–Joel Carillet: p. 14 (top); ©–ChrisVanLennepPhoto: p. 16 (top); ©–vernonwiley: p. 16 (bottom right); ©–RichVintage: p. 18; ©–Terry]: p. 19; ©–RyanJLane: p. 24. *Shutterstock, Inc.:* ©–Solid photos: p. 1; ©–Sergey Mironov: p. 7; ©–Dardalnna: pp. 8-9, 9 (top left); ©–Ronnie Chua: p. 9 (top right); ©–Trygve Finkelsen: p. 10 (top); ©–Martin Valigursky: p. 12; ©–KOTOTIMAGES: p. 13; ©–Konstantin Yolshin: p. 14 (bottom); ©–pjhpix: p. 15 (top); ©–PomInOz: p. 15 (bottom); ©–ChameleonsEye: p. 16; ©–Paya Mona: p. 16 (bottom left); ©–Evgeny Savchenko: p. 23. *Alamy:* ©–Rob Watkins: p. 3. *Dreamstime:* ©–Suzanne Tucker: p. 4 (top). *Photographed by Charles Clyde Ebbets:* pp. 20–21. *Tyrrell Photographic Collection, Powerhouse Museum:* p. 22.

ISBN: 978 1 3982 6016 0

British Library Cataloguing in Publication Data
A full catalogue record for this book is available from the British Library.

```
Printed and bound in India.
```

What do you like to do for fun? Gymnastics, skateboarding, cricket, ice hockey, skiing, swimming? These are all great hobbies, but they can be dangerous. Look out for the risks and you'll have a safe AND fun time.

Reading Road 2

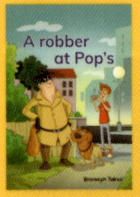

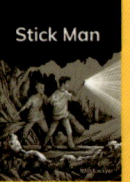

ISBN 978-1-3982-6016-0